Her
Forboden
Ikigai

a collection of short poems

Keyontaye Williams

Forboden Ikigai

Copyright © 2020 by keyontaye williams
All rights reserved

No part of this book may be used or reproduced in any manner **whatsoever** without written permission **except** in the case of reprints or in the context of reviews.

Editor ◆ keyontaye williams
Designer ◆ keyontaye williams

acknowledgements

amaranthine thanks to **GOD** for my continued journey

for which none of this would even be possible.

you have always known my heart and mind

and for that i am indebted to you

till times end.

and a special thanks, as always, to my loving mother

my sister, and to my beautiful daughter and son

who have been there for me every day

a special thanks goes to the rest of my family as well

who have continued to show me that even when

the shadows themselves overtake your light

the power to overcome them

exist within self always

thank you all

social media

Instagram ◆ kometigen

Twitter ◆ Progen

table of contents

Chapters

Σαγήνευση | Captivation   8

χάος από την ειρήνη | Chaos From Peace   120

Also From Author   162/184

About the Author   204

Experimental
texting box

experimental
write you own poems ✦✦✦ tell the world of your own amaranthine apologue in your own words

a quick warning.

this poetry book is straightforward, not necessarily reminiscent of ig

poetry, but lighter in that sense

if you are looking for something more dense and vocab heavy,

i recommend my "Amaranthine Apologue" series.

Enjoy

the readers mantra 《〉》 the writers decree

if beauty were love

we'd fall so easily

don't we know

i thought we knew

《〉》

to the writers of terrene

by the powers vested in we

I hereby decree

《〉》

for us, collectively, to give unto readers an opportunity to understand via love, what it took of us to manifest these amaranthine words of poetry, so that their world may continue to become the fiction our universe crafts as their reality; so that one day too, their knowledge of our love for them, can soon become what it takes to survive the tales that we ourselves could not survive alone; tales of a newly found purpose; a purpose soon becometh a writer found within themselves.....

Σαγήνευση
Captivation

Her Forboden Throwaways 《〉》 Forboden Ikigai

rodomontade
her cries of a metamorphic hide
unfolding the metamorphosis of her conquest
her words 《〉》 that of a sexual thunder
brash and loud
a tempest bravado of a desire for sin within her heart laid bare
wrestling with her demons in silent despair
wrestling where those swans of a feather flock
at the height of the encroachment
beneath the treasured cove
where she wrote literature of his truth within the diary that she kept
her forboden throwaways becometh her forboden ikigai
throwaways of her conception
throwaways of her blessing
a tale perfected 《〉》 but unprotected
the measure of her beauty
the wisdom of her medicine
forsaken
by a whispering wind of his resilience
his four-letter lexeme that taunts her still
casting shadows upon the canvas of her soul
remembrance of his stroke a lamenting memory
hued rust
haunting her as she runs further into a truth she pretends into reality

a reality of a phoenix risen from the ashes
the fleeting glimmers of a key to her liberation
as the hope within her dwindles
her silence begins a symphony in the depths of her soul
a symphony that weaves spells of solace
soothing the noise of his hurt into a solitude of quiet
forever entrenched is she now
within the clutches of her trauma
as she continues the literature
upon the reflective oasis of another new moon
the ikigai of her heart 《》 now too
the masterpiece of his hurt

💜 Vocabulary 💜

Forboden 《》 *a portmanteau of forbidden and forbode. implied to carry a sense of an ominous or foreboding prohibition; something that has been foretold as forbidden or ill-fated.*

Ikigai 《》 *is a japanese concept that refers to one's reason for being or the source of value in one's life that makes life worth living.*

Rodomontade 《》 *refers to boastful or extravagant bragging or bluster.*

The Virgin Mary

a goddess within her chrysalis
a tomb once unawakened
spells lift with the hint of a kiss
and the feel of his stroke
a cycle remiss of an actionable womb consumed with the glory of freedom
for whom ever may choose
dreams of the one who outmaneuvered her first imprint
as the walls of the virgin mary cave within through to the looms of a cocoon
forsaken by most

Liars Truth

he would cry to me
tears about how he could never lie to me
just to lie to me

Playing God

she played god by skipping stones
breaking hearts in the hopes of reaching her final form

HuN 《》 The Sweeter Tha Truth

it's not that you can do better hun
it's that you can do what's you
and i'm not you

Faith

i couldn't trust in you
so i had to have
faith

Trio

trio

you 《》 her 《》 me

the rest 《》 pleasant mysteries

in your eyes i see temptations

in my soul i see inundations

i've concentrated

waited for this moment

for the hour is ours

what to do

new moon will get the moans flowing

ready for action 《》 ready for excitement 《》 ready to incite it

but wait 《》 you make the first step

the deeper you gaze

the louder her praise

the longer the haze i'm lost within

i lo<3 your lips

i lo<3 your taste

when you could taste of me

subtle imagery all but a dream

as the knife behind my back

becomes a figment of reality

<u>**RM's Throwaways**</u>
The Forboden Chronicles
Chatper 1 《》 Amaranthine Chronicle

chronicled extra

read all about my life

amaranthine the enchantment that attracts

those to slow to escape the stenciled pain of their own remembrance

in the depths of my throwaways

Forboden Chronicle 《》 *write your forboden tale*

Chance and Choice Part 2: Good Mom

an ability to balance both his misfortunes
and the fortunes of your bairns inherited will of fire
simply can't exist
a choice at a chance for change
a chance squandered at your choice of tradition

Psychological Trauma 〈〉 Rape Kit

it's takes a lot for a man to be broken
it takes even more when a woman has a break in
to remain self

Obstacles in the Way

i don't know what obstacle is in the way of us not being in the
way of each other
but i do know
that i fear that if i learn your emotions
you'll be to bored to consider mine in return

Accountability

the problem with broken people is that
the struggles of life shouldn't make you so invincible
that you can't be held accountable

Prohibition

father
stale was he
a whisk of bourbon
a puff of smoke
an invigorated spirit of anger
and neglect
therapy of the soul begets a future unknown
but alas
the content creator of your imagining of self
prohibits you yet again

Cultural Shock

single mom shouted to me my affirmation
be the woman of the house
be everything your father never dreamed to become
so
alone i dreamt
dreams of our african history
dreams of our unity
dreams of our family
dreams of a planned division
dreams of pheromones controlling my senses
on what to become
leader of her ant hierarchy
succumbing to the hatred of a color
rather than the hatred of a bum

RM's Throwaways
The Forboden Chronicles
Chatper 2 《》 For Every Truth

damned if i do

damned if i don't

rosettes liter the landscape of a barren grave

what lies within may shock you

here in lies the reminiscent memories

of her forboden throwaways

stories of

the one that got away

Forboden Chronicle 《》 *write your forboden tale*

Auburn Autumn Snippet

"Just a few more minutes, and operation pentad goes into effect," Azariah uttered to herself with subtle disbelief. It had only been a month since their discovery of Auburn Autumn's journal and their journey inside of it. She still couldn't, no, she wouldn't allow herself to make sense of it. It was as if she had been lured into a dream; a dream from which she could never awaken.

As their mission slowly approached, she couldn't help but feel an abrupt uneasiness building deep within herself.

"What if they're all wrong and this doesn't work?"
"What if we can't circumvent death this time to bring her back?"
"What if... shit... it's time."

Azariah moved to her post like a thief in the night...

Pentad 《》 *a group of five.*

LGBT......

finding a life partner who's not just there for momentary
but there for the bigger picture
someone who's sole mission in life
is the betterment of you
someone who is your equal half of their own volition
and through your interpretation of what it means to be lo<3d
whether you be lesbian Δ bi Δ gay Δ trans
lo<3 is the equilibrium
hate is a chosen path necessary for balance in the natural order of
both good and evil abstractions
people will be born solely to hate you
to spite you at every chance
to hinder your achievements and manipulate your perspectives
when you are of your own conception
they will try to create your identity
to change the narrative of your existence to better equip their
own
you are not the products of a mental disease
you are not a way of life
you are not a phase
you are not their acceptable toleration levels
you are not the bonds of injustice that they have crafted
you are not a mistake Δ you are not unworthy
you are not the hell that they proclaim
you are the identity Δ the actualization Δ the animation
that you have always been

be proud of the light you walk within
and cast their stones of ignorance
into that of the un-weighted ponds of self-reflection

Eyes of the Wicked

cursed by eyes of wicked
attentive to her body
engulfed in the surroundings of her center
her soul is but a path thought of
but rarely acted upon

Perpetual Deviance

crafting mysterious images that only you can find

hide and seek champion

Dick Eater

consumer of a palette best served as a one night stand off

off of her game lately

who has she been of late

repetitious reactions to his late texts

as distressed veins stretch the latex

just in time for that late test

just in time

for her story's reimagining

Imagineer

primroses

tether round her forboden space

base form

three for one special

one birdie for every hole

evolutionary biology practitioners

RM's Throwaways
The Forboden Chronicles
Chatper 3 《 》 Loves Just a Secondhand Emotion

i can't love another

though i've tried

they always get in the way

of more of me

Forboden Chronicle 《》 *write your forboden tale*

The Taste of You

warm breath grazing
swollen pink lips
opened flower petals
dripping luscious nectar
tongue tip exploring
stirring inner fires
body trembling wildly
sweet juices flowing
thirst drinking deeply
the taste of you

softly teeth brushing
twitching crimson shaft
rock hard sculpture
chiseled from desire
silken lips accepting
coaxing forth eruption
hips thrusting quickly
thick essence exploding
throat swallowing greedily
the taste of me

bodies together facing
senses open expanding
nerves alive burning
feather touches tingling
mouths meeting crushing

tongues twisting mingling
salty sweet sharing
the taste of you
the taste of me
the taste of us

In Due Time

it wasn't a coincidence of fate that led us to one another
we were both deities
already having lived this life numerous times
we're just putting the pieces back where they belong
like all journey's
it takes temperament Δ invocation Δ maturation Δ experience

Ex_Tra

i think that i'm crazy for you

what

did you realize that after you inked my name into your skin…

psychotic acts of despair

Growth

she's the girl you meet when your reflection of self
has more to do with emotive understanding
and less to do with masculinity perpetuations

words of expression

Lo<3 Lost

if i had all the money in the world
the first thing i'd buy
is your assassination

                        scars of a broken heart

Coulrophobia

so many of you

at the cusp of your dreams

befriend yourself one of these

humor me this

wealth and awe

till the paint peels away

and its truth flakes within its flaws

RM's Throwaways
The Forboden Chronicles
Chatper 4 《》 Spades

ace in the hole

2nd times the charm

though expectant of other jokers tries

jokes on them every time

could never pierce my heart

less a spade come round and cut my veins as deeply as i do

will they

can they

bleed me dry to make me feel again

Forboden Chronicle 《》 *write your forboden tale*

Shoestrings

when i was just a young woman
my mother
who had been sitting by herself
called for me
so i waddled towards her
like a baby duck would its mother
my feet tripping over the laces of my new shoes with every step
as i made my way to the bathroom
still unsure as to her wanting need
she bent down and asked me
what is it that i told you about tying those shoestrings of yours
i hesitated for a moment
but then i responded
you told me that if i ever trip in life
it's because i wanted to but not because i needed to
i never forgot those words

Japanese Goldfish

i once had a beautiful japanese goldfish
it was a bright reddish orange color
it swam elegantly as if its bowl were an ocean
i fed it every day diligently as it slowly grew
my bond to the goldfish had increased
happy to be able to take care of something that was mine
but asleep i found myself to be on one strange night
a sudden thud in the night gave rise to suspicion
but i chose to ignore till my mother came in early that morning
her intentions pure
she had wanted to tell me something and then squish
she steps on my once beautiful japanese goldfish
how it got out of its fish bowl
till this day is a mystery to both my mother and me

Syndicate Relations

split tween red and blue will complicate your goals
till those purplish demons come and oxygenate your soul

Ambitions from Within

no one can make you who you're to become
you have to make yourself

the power from within

Impartial

you wanted fair

you wanted a man

you wanted dominance

crème brûlée was the position you spoke into existence for

yourself

and yet

you wanted to be three people

at the same time

Zoophagous

carnivorous beginnings
vegetated in unearthed meadows
arise vegan amidst summerys adventure

💜 Vocabulary 💜

Zoophagous 《》 *describes an organism or creature that feeds on animal matter or consumes other animals as part of its diet.*

RM's Throwaways
The Forboden Chronicles
Chatper 5 《》 Unauthorized Access Detected

still on the run

but i couldn't get away from you

im so scared of myself for not being so afraid of you

being tough to remain in charge of me

hiding pain inside of a strength you created

you scripted a versed version of a girl in transition to her

womanhood

forever locked away in a prison of your creation

dare i

give you a second chance to give me the key

to the first one

Forboden Chronicle 〈〉 *write your forboden tale*

Chalkzone

enough of your poems scribbled in rainbows
colored of the cosmic array
it is time now that i recreate my own destiny
my own destination scribbled with chalk
of a path fit for i

Length of a Sword

every battle isn't for everyone
though everyone can fight every battle

Derelict

i am but a derelict from a past long since forgotten

my purpose 《 》 unknown

i dig in the anamnesis that is our future

in hopes of bridging the gap between antecedent events

and fated destiny's

i've alternated however

continuums meant only to be contemplated instead

💜 Vocabulary 💜

Anamnesis 《 》 *the recollection or remembrance of the past; reminiscence.*

Derelict 《 》 *left or deserted, as by the owner or guardian; abandoned.*

Tale of OJ

you put me on this trial
because you wanted a black face
but the truth is
you never wanted a black voice

love's Song 《》 Once a Liar, Always a Thief

still i lie
skin sheds of old
love 《》 love 《》 love
the grass is greener as snake skins decompose
love 《》 love 《》 love
the sin taste just fine
come savor the bottle
chakras and ki bind
and still you'll never know

cause still i lie
still i lie
love 《》 love 《》 love

<u>RM's Throwaways</u>
The Forboden Chronicles
Chatper 6 《》 Over It

i'm over the what if's

what happened

happened

bygones be bygones

but what if...

Forboden Chronicle 《》 *write your forboden tale*

Itches of Pruriency

don't rub it
you're only going to tease the burn
don't ignore it
you're only going to stain the walls of your consciousness
with those flashbacks of desire and yearn
it just isn't the same if it isn't them
why train others when they know
why lie when it shows
leave over anything and start anew
only if you weren't theirs
only if you weren't crazy or psycho
this level of crazy breeds a new type of fear and realization
present moments are never what you envisioned
but lo<3s about patience

       that itch though

💜 Vocabulary 💜

Pruriency 《》 *refers to a state of being excessively interested in or preoccupied with sexual matters, often in a lustful or lewd manner.*

Life is a Box of Chocolates

she'd pondered about the loneliness of her emptiness inside
historians crafting a journey of her reminiscing manifestations
death to the dishonorable few that managed to hide truth of their beginnings
recreated in her box of chocolates those historians provide

Sadistic Passions

i remember waking up to you every morning
watching the morning light radiate off or your lips
thinking to myself how hurt you'd be
when you arose from your external shell and found your spirit
stuck
shocked at the mess i made

Synth

i pondered on a thought
a thought that you had already
like the wind synths of early morn

Your Harsh Words

your harsh words didnt hurt my feelings about self

they hurt my feelings about you

Chances Untaken

i dont want to take chances on people who dont want to take chances on me

Righteous Reaction

no brownie points for going off on people when they're wrong
we only go off when we're trying to do right

RM's Throwaways
The Forboden Chronicles
Chatper 7 《》 Womanhood Fiction

men

what are they good for

never met a girl i'd wife

that is until i met

you

Forboden Chronicle 《》 *write your forboden tale*

Generational Discon....

everyone else said fuck their kids
and then their kids said fuck themselves

Milford Mill

transporting memories
memories of our pubescence
young adolescents in charge
fully automated with not enough drive to spark their revolution
revolutions guided by those of power
statues of the older wars torn down
scapegoat be the bairn of their BLM agenda
how deep down the rabbit hole have they traveled to become
understood of self
from black ball to white ball
from blackmail to whitemail
from these feministic characteristics of cimmerian woes
subliminally imbued in their stories told anew
a new approach at our golden home
madagascar
a tall tale of a villain with flamboyant distinction
from divisive ordinances of black masculine via black feminine
the hetero male beget himself for eve's predisposition of self
her mirrored reflection of her apple
reflect within adam's inner inclinations
dress for success to literal to undermine
men in dresses
variegation of melanin forgoing their own for a taste of *****
tell me how far down the rabbit hole do you know
parks parked in a seat
perfect candidate for the job
forgo the pregnant

You and I

we used to be friends in love
our favorite times were sleepovers inside of our drugs
where did we go wrong
could it have been we consumed more than we sold
i know we just fell in love with the taste of hurt passions
i thought in you i could escape
but this is a lifestyle we chose

Truth Is

i never could see what you could dream
abstractions of our unspoken realities
actualized by peer pressure and memories of deceit
your words licked the knife you stuck inside of me
forever engaged in our criminality
gangsters of then tended their paradigms
for change
you
gangster of love
you tended mine in hopes of conformity
in hopes of discovering the new you of your own creation

Rest in Prognostication

an anachronistic progenitor was she

a monarch soaring high within these tellurian skys of our sovereignty

maternal in the wake of a newer life within her resplendent pilgrimage through time

you

her progeny

her paragon

the nonpareil animation of her manifest

shall carry her crown as her successor

and protect her throne as the true and new ranee

may she rest in prognostication

and may her memory never fade away from you

💜 Vocabulary 💜

Nonpareil 《》 *means having no equal, unrivaled, or unparalleled.*

Prognostication 《》 *refers to the act of predicting or forecasting future events or outcomes based on present indications, trends, or knowledge.*

Ranee 《》 *refers to a queen or a female ruler, especially in south asia.*

RM's Throwaways
The Forboden Chronicles
Chapter 8 《》 Dom

show me a tick of two

as i run away from

a past that wants badly

to be my forever future

Forboden Chronicle 《》 *write your forboden tale*

The Forgotten Carnation of Yen

motley montage

carnations of yen

forgotten

her mintage revitalizing pictorials of lovers in the recesses of her

mind

on a double-sided coin

one which spins soul ties

and threads them

to a coarse heart

a heart

out of time

Next Stop

contemplating us on those mta days

days where the will for a drive within myself felt automated

outside of my control at times

swerving obstacles and our constant pitstops

in avoidance of the worst things about our present inclinations

inclinations of two lovers

on the run

from one another

towards a dream of something better that has yet to come

Happy Feet

remembrance of when
disagreements led to the loss of friends
argumentative predispositions that
with time
we could soon amend
and now
they just shoot you in your feet
with the hopes that you never
walk again

Prime Chasity Postpubescence

as humble as we are now
there's still suspense of our beginnings
daydreams of their suspicion
tell me
what is this feeling
this undeniable feeling of titillation
where once
i was your superman
and you
you were my femme fatale
where the cloaks round our waist
represented the prime chastity of our postpubescence

<u>RM's Throwaways</u>
The Forboden Chronicles
Chapter 9 《》 Body Scan

>a lascivious bit..
>
>but only for you
>
>you catch me when i fall
>
>out of love again
>
>who though
>
>will catch me when i find
>
>me

Forboden Chronicle 《》 *write your forboden tale*

Oceanic Pleasure

the real truth of your ocean is the deeper i sink
the more that i let in
the more we make lo<3
the more you resent
but the more i feed on your inner inclination
the more you're content

Danyia and Iviris Snippet

The party itself served merely as a distraction; its focal point: Danyia Ruel, also known as Iviris's ex. Danyia's departure from Iviris stemmed from the nature of her inclinations; it wasn't a detail I invited you here to dwell upon. No, I brought you here for something far more sinister.

The story begins with Danyia entering the party, as if in search of someone. Amidst the cacophony of voices and music, a familiar shout pierces through.

Linfrey: Yo, Dani! Dani!

Dani scans the crowd, eventually locating the source: Linfrey, or as she used to call him, "Fre." They shared an art class in high school, though that seemed like eons ago.

Dani: Fre?

Danyia's shock is palpable as she sees Linfrey after so many years. He appears markedly different now, having matured both aesthetically and physically.

Linfrey: Yes, yes. I know. It's the hair, isn't it? Just a little change and people lose their minds, you know, heheh.

Danyia: Yeah, I know what you mean... Hey listen, you wouldn't happen to know where she is, would you?

Linfrey, already sensing the subject of their conversation, smiles and gestures toward a spiral staircase.

Danyia: Oh... Thanks, Fre.

Linfrey: Yeah, sure, no problem. And it's not Fre.

Their eyes meet one last time, sharing a moment of sincere laughter, before Danyia disappears into the crowd, retracing steps to a past unforgotten.

Things You Can't Change

hydrant filled tensions

reveal pent lust

busting at the seams

the heart wants what the heart wants

Pillow Talks of East and West

Boy: If I would have made lo<3 to you that day, it wouldn't have even mattered, because you would have still been in lo<3 with him

Woman: If I would have made lo<3 to you that day, it wouldn't have even mattered, because you would have still been in lo<3 with you.

Squirt Squirt: Forboden Tales of the Wap

she had once yearned for his exciting rage
displayed was it on her face
a wicked painter and his canvas
wet dreams actualized
a curved dagger sheathed
was what she thought she desired most
something intoxicating
she never could of imagined that
something real
could feel like plastic
a foreign taint of the girl she could never return to

RM's Throwaways
The Forboden Chronicles
Chatper 10 《》 Our Throwaways

love with an asterisk attached

you date what you can't have

but you know that I need of you

i mean who will I run too

when you find that you need

only you

Forboden Chronicle ⟨⟩ *write your forboden tale*

Vision

i kept seeing what it was we could have been

i just never got around to asking if we could have been

Gunsmoke and Dreams unfulfilled

how could he do that to me

she would ask herself

why would he go against our promise

sure she had things his new girl didn't have

but those things

those things aren't what he's there for

trying to recreate her inside of her

as the immaterial immaturity sets in

so to

does the gun smoke fill the dream-esque atmosphere

Spookasem

shape of peach

but taste as yummy as a carnival in july

💜 Vocabulary 💜

Spookasem 《》 *an afrikaans term that translates to "cotton candy" in english.*

Indomitable Liberation

i'm a freedom fighter

i don't ignite the spark just to hide in the shadows

♥ Vocabulary ♥

Indomitable ⟨⟩ *means unable to be subdued, conquered, or overcome; unbeatable, unyielding, or invincible.*

Nasty Thoughts

inducing overwhelming climaxes of my ideologies inside of your cogitation
that impregnate your cerebration with wet dreams of my overflowing imagination
out of your mouth flow a thousand etymologies of many a contemplation
the spit dripping off the length of my floccinaucinihilipilification is quite devastating
you need a moment to process your sudden hesitation
understanding of knowledge in self is complicating
hidden temptation of freaky dictions in vulvas
the au fait of the stroke is amazing
the ichorous liquids pumping throughout your inner station…

💜 Vocabulary 💜

Au Fait 《》 *having experience or practical knowledge of a thing; expert; versed.*
Floccinaucinihilipilification 《》 *the estimation of something as valueless.*
Ichorous 《》 *an ethereal fluid flowing in the veins of the gods.*

RM's Throwaways
The Forboden Chronicles
Chatper 11-12 《》 Can You Keep a Secret | Dickery

the puddle you manifest between my legs

it yearns for completion

it yearns for therapy

it yearns

for dick

fuck

im sorry ok

it was one time

I promise

i promise that im yours

only yours

Forboden Chronicle 《》 *write your forboden tale*

Textual Pt 1

hey
sorry about earlier
moms called about family dinner tonight
have to cancel

WestWorld

anachronistic progenitors

besting being created by their oppressors

to becoming their creators

Phrenic Necrosis

she lives to die everyday

that's why she prays

in the hope that you'll see her

before her dying embrace

💜 Vocabulary 💜

Phrenic ⟨⟩ relates to the diaphragm, which is the major muscle involved in breathing, located below the lungs and heart.

Aemarêy and Emory: Snippet

Emory: How many dainty stars are there?

Aemarêy: I'd say infinity if I had to guess.

Aemarêy and Emory are on the floor in Emory's room, looking at the star-studded ceiling. As they both smoke a long spliff, they begin to reminisce over memories of the past. Once upon a time, they had something special with one another, but those times have long since passed.

There are three specific stars on the ceiling, all of which are missing pieces, that catch Aemarêy's attention.

Aemarêy: I remember that star, the one in the top right corner, with the crooked tip, I mean.

Emory turns to look at Aemarêy, her lips slowly pursing together to form a sincere smile.

Aemarêy: That was when you and I... Well... Yeah...

Emory, pausing mid-smoke with Aemarêy, eyes her with a glaring stare as if attempting to look into her soul. Acmarêy, sensing the intent behind the look, is the first to break away. Both girls laugh at each other. Aemarêy, still in a trance of sorts, has Haimes on her mind, a boy she's just met and for whom she has also fallen. Not knowing what to do or say, she offers her words on the matter.

Aemarêy: Look, I know it's your get-together and everything, and how you still feel about me, and I wouldn't want that to get in the way of our friendship, you know.

Emory, now fully engaged, tries to play it off as if nothing's wrong.

Emory: Why would anything ever come between us?

Aemarêy: Good.

Aemarêy, now walking around the room, picks up a musical box and begins to open it slowly, deep in thought.

Aemarêy: I invited him, Haimes that is, to this little soiree of sorts if you want to call it that. That's why I even brought it up. I didn't want to make you uncomfortable, that's all.

Emory, now slightly annoyed, asks Aemarêy the question she can no longer hold back.

Emory: Why Haimes?

Aemarêy sets down the music box as if her high has just been disrupted.

Aemarêy: This again? I knew being around each other would be a mistake. It's always the same with you, Emory. You have to let us go.

Aemarêy starts to head for the door and exits Emory's room, and Emory runs after her to convince her that she's sorry.

Emory: Ae, wait up…

RM's Throwaways
The Forboden Chronicles
Chatper 13-14 ⟨⟩ Our Throwaways: Painful Gain | White and Black

                                                              your pain my gain

                                the more that i wither away over you

                    the more that the petals you had once blossomed

                                          lose their pigmentation

                                  i think i'm beginning to see

                                              the you in me

you're family ties destructive of me

they have hatred for me

disgusted by the nature of me

why'd i lend credence to their traumas over the understanding of my own

i guess together

we will see

Forboden Chronicle 《》 *write your forboden tale*

Textual Pt 2

> *so i was able to come up with a lie*
> *it's still on*
> *i'm so happy*
> *i love you*

Get Another Clue

innocent eyes pry
popcorn ceiling
a loss of innocence
daydreams fulfilling real dreams
the reality you wished
never arrives in rural counties like ours

Matriarch

your mom
it started with her
the inklings of history
repair themselves yet again
equipped with your beauty
whilst immersed in your authenticity

Hammonds 2nd Mistake

why create one island

when you can make more

BDSM

i can lift you with my voice then there's no need to beat you
if i can flick you with my tongue then there's really no need for words
if I can visualize your pain then our heart is see through
because the essence of our scars is ingrained inside of these cryptic shores tidal waving at the bat of an eye
if they escape
let it be as secretive as the bud of your burgeoning womanhood
risking a glimpse of freedom
for a tempting sensation to lead her astray

Textual Pt 3

*silly i cant get on facetime right now
still getting ready
gonna sneak out after the family
gets together*

The Devils Propaganda

the devils working
all he ever needed was the pen
anything beats a life of death and sin
allegorical was my oracle for eons on end

Secretive

the transcendence of my dreams
bleeding through to our reality
wondering
if the gods above speak of our activities
sorting through our encephalon's
as does an author bookmarking their journey
ready to soon return yet again

💜 Vocabulary 💜

Encephalon 《》 *is the entire contents of the skull, including the brain, spinal cord, and associated membranes, but more commonly, it refers specifically to the brain.*

<u>RM's Throwaways</u>
The Forboden Chronicles
Chatper 15-16 《》 Type of Tears | Hospital i Call Home

swaying in the breeze

over top my body

strung out over a barren grave

slumberland amidst the one i love

tricky thing about the rose you adorned

is the prickly thorns that grow from within

Forboden Chronicle 《》 *write your forboden tale*

Tres

they say fool me once

shame on you

fool me twice

shame on you

fool me three times

amaranthine apologues of

rosaceae manke

the one that didn't get away

Checks Up on The Kid

Boy: You've been checking everything I do for self.
Boy: What, you think I'm mad?

Woman: "I think sending 'checks' instead of cash would probably make you mad, like, checks up on his kid; puts checks on top of checks on top of checks up for the bibs, the diapers and the crib; checks for education and the way that your baby lives; checks on the mother of his child; checks to see that she's straight; checks to make sure that they have bread and linen on their plates; checks for pleasuring when the father of my child is the man I pleasured in, don't want to resent; checks for family orientation; checks for my family both out of lo<3 and when we make it; checks for the anniversary of when we made we, her."

Textual 4

> *where are you*
> *i'm here at out spot*
> *it's cold*
> *very cold*

4th Wall

still in love with a ghost i see

she still has all of his love letters

an ode to an amaranthine apologue as good as theirs

makes her bleed past this fourth wall of life

in hopes of joining him in a world past death

Prāyaścitta

mistress

wife

lover

sex slave

nude buttocks hoisted

a swing built for entrapment

her arms and hands bound behind her backside

all entry wounds scarred from failed expectations

prāyaścitta soon to was her manifest

blindfolded to hide herself from herself

though she could not hide from his unsheathed manhood

a newer truth she'd let consume her

healing those wounds with an alabaster remedy

one which her facial expressions

were once again

delighted to experience

💜 Vocabulary 💜

Prāyaścitta ⟨⟩ *is a sanskrit term from hinduism and jainism that refers to an act of penance, expiation, or atonement performed by an individual to cleanse themselves of sins or wrongdoings.*

RM's Throwaways
The Forboden Chronicles
Chatper 17-18 《》 Nurse Joy | Memory

                                                i awaken to the sound of music

                                                  it plays a subtle poetry

                                          i love the rhythm of its notes

                    as they harmoniously blend with the sounds of my world

                                      channeling channels i blocked

                                              channels that still

                                                        haunt me

nurse …

nurse…

nurse…

he's breathing into me

nurse…

it's okay

i think it was just another dream

my name is nurse joy

i'll be taking care of you for now

Forboden Chronicle 《》 *write your forboden tale*

Textual 5

> oh i see you
> finally you're here
> lol
> i missed you

Fairytales Dreams

fairytale dreams of immaculate conceptions
conceptualized by false realities that once slept
just to awake as mere illusions bound by no plot
tales of a darker romance
souls lost through the intertwined fragments of broken promises
and repaired hearts that were never broken
they break
fractured pieces reshaping a delicate balance
a balance that was never really fixed from the start

Answers

after you

i could never want for more

your energy for which i yearn

completes my inner equilibrium

a natural balance that intruded upon gates closed to outside forces

and still

you infected me

your temptation persuades me

yes

when the answer should be no

Paroxysm

the flood gates

unbearable
uncontrollable
unrelenting

💜 Vocabulary 💜

Paroxysm 《》 *a sudden attack or violent expression of an emotion or activity. Hysteria.*

RM's Throwaways
The Forboden Chronicles
Chatper 19-20 ⟪⟫ Our Throwaways: Meant For Another | Medical

trying to heal what's left in this barren wasteland

only thing left is your heart

but maybe

just maybe

our love will escape

a week in this psych ward yet again

i don't miss my responsibilities

only you that i miss

Forboden Chronicle 《》 *write your forboden tale*

χάος από την ειρήνη

Chaos From Peace

Her Forboden Throwaways 《》 Captivate Your Audience

i mean

what more can i say to persuade them
if i've already bled out profusely
they've boiled her poison within me
hoping to gauge the extent of our misery
hoping to gauge her love for me
though
it was a loveless commitment
one man's fate bestowed onto another
she threw her inner god away
way before i came round
why wallow over flag colors
they all end posted in the ground
so i played a role scripted for a few before me
not used to this societal arena
the option to be fated
whatever happened to soulmates
whatever happened to happily ever after
now it's shadows of deceit
i'm merely a turn
this ferris wheel is slower that most
yet ends all the same
i look into her eyes and see
the war to get out of this
it was there ever since i arrived

the opportunity to see beauty in others
just to hold them as placeholders for my replacement
thought that i was your trifecta
now these fragments are what excite you
but then again
none of them are me
and i'm not her
i never wanted to be
but then you knew
you always knew

Thug Passion

she was unaware of his secret
though she would need it
he had on his
butters
grey sweats
a white beater
and the heat under his polo jacket was anemic
she had on Victoria's secret
and even still she couldn't keep it
thought she would
thought she could
her nervous jitters aroused in her
a fiery excitement
a pleasured delight
dripping from the brows beneath her sanctuary

Textual 6

> HOW COULD YOU
> YOU SAID THAT YOU LOVED ME
> THAT I WAS DIFFERENT
> THAT I WAS SPECIAL

Make Me Cu#

droplets trickling down
as does the dew of a leafy branch
sticky the amber honey glaze
pollinated by the breadth of the northern flicker

Anuran Serpents of Prevarication

land ho 《》 roman 《》 woman 《》 satan 《》 satin sheets
lost with alice in the scheme of things
annuna gods awaken in a dream of sleep
as the snake speaks the fear swarms we've lost GOD in a sin storm
we've lost values
morales too
our pyramidal structures imbued with eyes of heru
erections lesson to the large intestine
masculinity who we pretend to be
the tendency for making unitary energy of the same sex identity
the resurrection of a celestial entity

💜 Vocabulary 💜

Annuna 《》 the highest gods in the mesopotamian pantheon.

Anuran 《》 any amphibian of the order anura, comprising the frogs and toads.

Heru 《》 a sky god who was one of the oldest gods of ancient egypt.

RM's Throwaways
The Forboden Chronicles
Chatper 21-23 《》 Release Me | Our Throwaways: Imprisonment | Department of Corrections: John Doe

                the rain always meshes with the tears i drop

    how long was it ago when i discovered how to disguise my pain inside of

                                            yours

    seems i've finally been able to peer inside the secrets you too keep hidden

                          and you dare to peer into mine

if its anything a nurse knows

its how to mend the wounds of fallen soldiers

i've fallen for many

too many to reconcile there and then

nor here and again

                                        felonious crimes

                                  to be free or not to be

                                  one thing is for certain

                                  i'll never let you go

Forboden Chronicle 《》 *write your forboden tale*

Protection

if it weren't for russell marker

there'd be wombs of desolation

poems

stories

and raps of malaise

about many a situation

always use protection

Callipygian

when i'm graced with your presence
i can't help but notice a brilliant truth
when you walk away from me
your derrière has this sudden power over me
a power that sways me to follow you
as a light does a shadow

💜 Vocabulary 💜

Callipygian 〈〉 *having well-shaped buttocks.*

Sicko Mode

she was used to shaving her plantation
for others platoons to succumb too

Abendrot

a perfect setting for a sanguine love as ours

❤ Vocabulary ❤

Abendrot 〈〉 is a german word that means "evening redness" or "the reddish glow of the sky at sunset."

Writers Block

search deep
inside of your mental faculties
to find that part of you
that giveth us stories authenticated
by the genius within

Deletion

she told him how she thought it impossible to leave
her tattoos of his heart on her sleeve
transcended from emotions to emotive imprints
never again
able to feel
alone

Cucumber Challenge

they song of you
the girl in aisle ten
the girl unafraid of the glory of her truth
as the firmness of her succelent lips
produce an adhesive mixture of trust and experience
and caress the produce
permeating a glory hole of her own creation

<u>**RM's Throwaways**</u>
The Forboden Chronicles
Chatper 24-26 《》 Dream Walking | Our Throwaways: Auburn Autumn | Department of Corrections: Byrd

who is this woman

this woman that loves me so

is she a figment of now or more to come

can she heal me

or will she destroy what's left

you've known me

my name

my work

my love for you

how could you not remember

your fragrance still smells of pepper spray

you're giving me felonious energy

why the fragmented mental

Forboden Chronicle 《》 *write your forboden tale*

Jail Bait 《》 Soothing Tenderness

told you i loved putting my head on your chest in our early days
as you heard of my thug filled sorrows
sorrows birthed in those streets that never claimed me worthy
i grew deeper into the rabitt hole that gave me courage
though i must admit
those nipples the size of tootsie rolls
the way they'd caress my tears away
they provided shelter for my rainy days
i was so young back then
questioning what it was you wanted with me
even fell into the trap of sin
called me your

Soupçon

it's our moment

don't become my world in a moment of time

and i promise not to become yours

you're not here for titles or first loves

your first love was yourself

promise not to become yours

promise just to experience a little bit of you

you're here to fuck

and get fucked

to give that macaroni salad purpose yet again

Forgiveness

i miss the shit that was real
not the temptations that were in-between us
as i reimagine my tongue in-between us
thinking back to a time were what was yours
had once belonged to me

Anamorphic Temptation

the verity of her prevarication is akin to sin
licentious in her barren skin
she's inveigled the veridicality of many virtuous women and men
she inveigled he 《〉》 esoteric in her cerebration
imaginations of her flagitious smile turned thoughts of a tongue
swirling round and round
estuaries of tongue and pudendum adjoin
as it floods her isthmus a chersonese appears
mucilaginous exudations 《〉》 athirst agitations
let her feed you
but wait it's just that you don't know of us
my name is anamorphic
her name is ___
and her name is her
it's nice to meet you
what's your name ○● oh
you're temptation
a foundational lust for her contem…
ssshhh…
silence
aphonic
temptation you gormandizer
you are the wiser
___ words mean less with an apogeic conquest
ethereal aviation 《〉》 aerial aerobatics
as you lift her past your encephalon
sky dine

clenching her epidermis 《》 her clenches back
legs interlaced 《》 scarifications of a close encounter
lay her on the counter
wait 《》 just wait 《》 just wait
i've had enough
emanations of ___ animalism lead to amaurosis
i'm abstract
her corporal frame is aphrodisiac
oh 《》 my 《》 god
temptations weapon of infliction is near
there's no time to waste
___ succulent bud given a taste
another succulent bud caught in a grasp of no escape
salivary napes of poignancy
no interregnums
i'm losing control
her and ___ are combining forces
 trichotomic extortions 《》 only if i allow
the osculate of the napes simmer down
as i rebound i think an anamnesis
a couple of temptations from way before
the last temptation ___ gave in
this temptation was supposed to settle the score
she's not strong enough
so i anamorphic
will put a st…
ssshhh…
silence
aphonic
commodious is temptations hidden feature

a copious encephalon of great measure

💜 Vocabulary 💜

Amaurosis ⟨⟩ *partial or total loss of sight, especially in the absence of a gross lesion or injury.*
Anamnesis ⟨⟩ *recollection of the ideas, which the soul had known in a previous existence, especially by means of reasoning.*
Anamorphic ⟨⟩ *having or producing unequal magnifications along two axes perpendicular to each other.*
Aphonic ⟨⟩ *lacking phonation; unvoiced.*
Aphrodisiac ⟨⟩ *an aphrodisiac food, drug, potion, or other agent that arouses sexual desire.*
Apogeic ⟨⟩ *the highest or most distant point; climax.*
Chersonese ⟨⟩ *a peninsula.*
Commodious ⟨⟩ *spacious and convenient; roomy.*
Encephalon ⟨⟩ *the brain*
Estuary ⟨⟩ *that part of the mouth or lower course of a river in which the river's current meets the seal's tide.*
Flagitious ⟨⟩ *shamefully wicked as persons, actions, or times.*
Gormandizer ⟨⟩ *to eat greedily or ravenously.*
Interregnums ⟨⟩ *an interval of time between the sovereigns reign and the accession of his or her normal or legitimate successor.*
Licentious ⟨⟩ *sexually unrestrained; lascivious; libertine; lewd.*
Mucilaginous ⟨⟩ *adhesive.*
Trichotomic ⟨⟩ *the three-part division of human beings in body, spirit, and soul.*
Verity ⟨⟩ *the state or quality of being true; accordance with fact or reality.*

Dvandva Exordium from the Deep

the covetousness beginning of the truth in my lies has left me to
feel rather
bittersweet
a lonesome monopoly over yours
you're mythological outcome of you and me becoming a
wholesome we
how these dvandva exordiums runeth amuck deep within
agog in their efforts to overwhelm
see
you were his before you ever were mine
as i ponder pain and rhyme
the sorrows of the clementine rose
of the spring summery and mine intertwine
wafting in its aroma
still frozen from the wintertide
my insides
freezer–burned
from the hidden lust kept on the other side

💜 Vocabulary 💜

Agog 《》 *excited by eagerness, curiosity, anticipation, etc.*
Clementine Rose °•° *light, sparkling wine cultivated by coeur clémentine.*
Covetousness 《》 *inordinately or wrongly desirous of wealth or possessions; greedy.*
Dvandva 《》 *a compound word neither element of which is subordinate to the other, as anglo-saxon.*

Exordium 《〉》 *the beginning of anything.*
           Wintertide 《〉》 *Wintertime.*

Lissome
Erotica
Tootsie Slide

lissome lithes be her name
mental erotica
made with lavender
sensual challenger | sexual astonisher
that new tootsie slide
becomes standing stances that turn into splits
a freak of nature all on her own
the type to never bring home
home alone with myself
i'm mental enough for myself
she's sexual tension all on her own
i'm here for her all on my own

💜 Vocabulary 💜

Lithesome 《》 *or lithe, especially of body; supple; flexible.*

<u>RM's Throwaways</u>
The Forboden Chronicles
Chatper 27-29 《》 Department of Corrections: Paige | Department of Corrections: Maple and Chaplin | Department of Corrections: Grape Street Crip

page from his notebook

first day home

mother told me about boys like you

shame i never listened

maple and chaplin

where first we met

where first they took you away from me

where first we met

again

the feelings strange

the street let you rot

yet you made wine from grapes

Forboden Chronicle 《》 *write your forboden tale*

Chance and Choice Part 1: Good Mom

an ability to balance both his misfortunes
and the fortunes of your bairns inherited will of fire
simply can't exist
a choice at a chance for change
a chance squandered at your choice of tradition

Sting

she used his trauma
to disguise being healed
lying to herself
to remember the sting she left behind

Immorality

she used to ask me if my mortality matter more to me than my immortality

Ecoanxiety ⟨⟩ The Soul-Tie That Binds

anachronistic souls through life
procreative villages imbued with tradition
environmental alters produce with conviction
a life sentence stained with tears of cum
just enough for a face beat with a forboden magic
just enough magic
creeping in before their ejected method of protection

Anachronistic ⟨⟩ *describes something that is out of its proper time period, often appearing to belong to an earlier era.*

Ecoanxiety ⟨⟩ *refers to a psychological or emotional state characterized by feelings of worry, fear, or stress related to environmental issues, such as climate change, pollution, habitat destruction, or loss of biodiversity.*

Facedown part 1 《》 the Inescapable Hog-Tie

heat wave consumes

droplets of sexual tension becometh astral fumes

imbued with the vigor of min

contempt in the veracity of men

attitudinal adjustments in play

drupe form candied

as yellow as the tint of your hue

ripened smacks as red as the maturation of your redolence

your lips sealed

archivist of your secrets

as the serpent that slithers flickers its tongue

and the truth-seeking rod reciprocates the facade of your stubborn pride

your hidden mist becometh revealed from behind your veiled treasure cove*

seems like she's ready

ready for perforation

the truth of the lioness caged within

readily available for the serpents sin

the serpent knows your truth

an antidote for the scars that form anew amid your tempted frustrations

from your inner thighs

to your sensuous extremities

those succulent toes

color coded white for a blacked occasion

voluptuous thighs

bonded tight for the occasion
your barren legs
paradigmatic for an unbeknownst erection a-knockin at the
entrance to your humble abode
no locked doors
no way to escape it
the serpent's erection slithering its way deep within your inner
proclivity
as your daydreams align with realities constant measure
a sigh of a pleasured release escapes the depths of your soul...

RM's Throwaways
The Forboden Chronicles
Chatper 30 《》 Fuck The System

fuck the system
what did it ever do for me
i trusted him
the system trusted him too
in tears
my scars my own
my story my own
the ikigai of my fears
eternal within my forboden chronicles

Glossary

Abendrot ⟨⟩ is a german word that means "evening redness" or "the reddish glow of the sky at sunset."

Agog ⟨⟩ excited by eagerness, curiosity, anticipation, etc.

Amaurosis ⟨⟩ partial or total loss of sight, especially in the absence of a gross lesion or injury.

Anachronistic ⟨⟩ describes something that is out of its proper time period, often appearing to belong to an earlier era.

Anamnesis ⟨⟩ the recollection or remembrance of the past; reminiscence.

Anamorphic ⟨⟩ having or producing unequal magnifications along two axes perpendicular to each other.

Annuna ⟨⟩ the highest gods in the mesopotamian pantheon.

Anuran ⟨⟩ any amphibian of the order anura, comprising the frogs and toads.

Aphonic ⟨⟩ *lacking phonation; unvoiced.*

Aphrodisiac ⟨⟩ *an aphrodisiac food, drug, potion, or other agent that arouses sexual desire.*

Apogeic ⟨⟩ *the highest or most distant point; climax.*

Au Fait ⟨⟩ *having experience or practical knowledge of a thing; expert; versed.*

Callipygian ⟨⟩ *having well-shaped buttocks.*

Chersonese ⟨⟩ *a peninsula.*

Clementine Rose ∘•∘ *light, sparkling wine cultivated by coeur clémentine.*

Commodious ⟨⟩ *spacious and convenient; roomy.*

Covetousness ⟨⟩ *inordinately or wrongly desirous of wealth or possessions; greedy.*

Derelict ⟨⟩ *left or deserted, as by the owner or guardian; abandoned.*

Dvandva ⟨⟩ *a compound word neither element of which is* *subordinate to the other, as anglo-saxon.*

Ecoanxiety 《》 *refers to a psychological or emotional state characterized by feelings of worry, fear, or stress related to environmental issues, such as climate change, pollution, habitat destruction, or loss of biodiversity.*

Encephalon 《》 *is the entire contents of the skull, including the brain, spinal cord, and associated membranes, but more commonly, it refers specifically to the brain.*

Estuary 《》 *that part of the mouth or lower course of a river in which the river's current meets the seal's tide.*

Exordium 《》 *the beginning of anything.*

Flagitious 《》 *shamefully wicked as persons, actions, or times.*

Floccinaucinihilipilification 《》 *the estimation of something as valueless.*

Forboden 《》 *a portmanteau of forbidden and forbode. implied to carry a sense of an ominous or foreboding prohibition; something that has been foretold as forbidden or ill-fated.*

Gormandizer 《》 *to eat greedily or ravenously.*

Heru 《》 *a sky god who was one of the oldest gods of ancient egypt*

Ichorous 《》 *an ethereal fluid flowing in the veins of the gods.*

Ikigai 《》 *is a japanese concept that refers to one's reason for being or the source of value in one's life that makes life worth living.*

Indomitable 《》 *means unable to be subdued, conquered, or overcome; unbeatable, unyielding, or invincible.*

Interregnums 《》 *an interval of time between the sovereigns reign and the accession of his or her normal or legitimate successor.*

Licentious 《》 *sexually unrestrained; lascivious; libertine; lewd.*

Lithesome 《》 *or lithe, especially of body; supple; flexible.*

Mucilaginous 《》 *adhesive.*

Nonparell 《》 *means having no equal, unrivaled, or unparalleled.*

Paroxysm 《》 *a sudden attack or violent expression of an emotion or activity. Hysteria.*

Pentad 《》 *a group of five.*

Phrenic ⟨⟩ relates to the diaphragm, which is the major muscle involved in breathing, located below the lungs and heart.

Prognostication ⟨⟩ *refers to the act of predicting or forecasting future events or outcomes based on present indications, trends, or knowledge.*

Pruriency ⟨⟩ *refers to a state of being excessively interested in or preoccupied with sexual matters, often in a lustful or lewd manner.*

Ranee ⟨⟩ *refers to a queen or a female ruler, especially in south asia.*

Rodomontade ⟨⟩ *refers to boastful or extravagant bragging or bluster.*

Spookasem ⟨⟩ *an afrikaans term that translates to "cotton candy" in english.*

Trichotomic ⟨⟩ *the three-part division of human beings in body, spirit, and soul.*

Verity ⟨⟩ *the state or quality of being true; accordance with fact or reality.*

Wintertide ⟨⟩ *Wintertime.*

Zoophagous 《》 *describes an organism or creature that feeds on animal matter or consumes other animals as part of its diet.*

Also From Author

Rabbit Hole of Choice and Chance

if i say nothing then it's because of pride

if i say anything then it's full of lies

if i don't try enough then i've lost us

and even when i do try you're still cuffed to the very same lust

that had once attracted you to me ∆ you weren't here for lo<3

you were mean in our beginning

that gave you full authority over me

but i had something that you needed

that allowed me complete dominion over you

a subtle balance

but without it what was i but a mere hookup on the cusp of

breakups and regressions

no more chances upon chances ∆ no more begging ∆ no more

cheats

i hate cheats that lie of crazed temptations

only to persuade illustrious illusions of a rabbit hole

its mysteries i fall for every time

- *chains of temptation*

Lo<3 Letter #4

you fell in lo<3 with the idea of me but never of we

i balanced mistakes of past to make a better imagery

you wanted my mind to continue but our lo<3 to cease

you gave me conflict before there ever was peace

i gave you lo<3 before there ever was hate

you gained everything from me now there's nothing to take

i gave you life before death could even awake

you dreamt of a dream dreamt out of devil's fate

i dreamt a deck of lies

a licentious queen of reap

you governed my momentary lapse of reality

my biased predilections of an i'm perfection

you figure i learned my lesson

left me with lustful regressions

before my conversion to love could make a lasting impression

i figure my many affections

ignorantly given because of my niceties

no need in stressing

because even when you doubted me

you're finally where you thought

i'd be

alone

sincerely

my last broken trust of loyalty

Prologue

"On the eve of October 23, 1996, an anachronistic phantasm of lyrics through time is what she appeared to me as."

"A reverie of an abstracted inamorata who promised of a euphoric escape from the many chimeras of my distant past, is how she lured me into believing her to be the mystery in which i thought to be true. But, how foolishly wrong i had been."

"it wasn't evident to me at the time, nor was i aware of the imminent demise of those closest to me, but one thing was for certain; she was not who she had claimed herself to be."

"She was...

evil."

"My death, as well as the deaths of those closet to me, was what 'she' had take from us; was what she had taken from me."

"But this isn't a story of how we lost it all, no. Not even close."

"My name, is Azariah Rose, and this is a story of our truth; a story of her villainy; a story of my revenge."

Fata Morgana ∆ Apples of Moira

at the cusp of our dreams lies a bigger fallacy asleep

as our apple awaits

the ignis fatuus of fate speaks

the world was you and your world was a lie

your world soon became us two and it became our truth

fools once were we

and now

irregular energies we are

stuck in an uncommon domain of lo<3

Faceted Amorous

i was drawn to her faceted amorous on the canvas of my
mental cogitation her animus lit like cannabis
contemplating my animalia matrix of duplicating originations
i began reimagining imaginations of self which formulated our
present stasis
i was integral inside of her confrontational status
at first an incumbent but anon awoken within my metian
apparatus
while she envisaged chess games of snakes and ladders
i astral projected self-past her envisagement of snakes for the
latter

Deuces

i'd be wrong if i said i've lo<3d better

i still have all of your lo<3 letters

after all the times you hurt me

thought i would have learned better but you were clever

turned me against myself Δ turned me into jealousy

stressed out and rebellious how could i ever tell you this

i was in lo<3 remember

the day that you told me that was my own december

we were on trent street

i was all alone staring at the street sign and somehow i still

couldn't give it the peace sign

we've both run out of lust Δ we've both run out of luck

but how could i ever chuck the deuce when i still give a f...

- just.let.go

Xenophilic Erudition · Letters To Our Oppressor

the quandary that pothers the deontology of americanized
privilege enucleates itself of its amorphous shell of cultural
appropriation ·
appropriation · the indefatigable nostrum of our oppressors
paradigm ·
was an exigency birthed out of necessity and cogitation
the abstruse dictation of other cultures and ethnic groups in
the hopes of appropriating their customs and traditions
allowing for the re-enslavement of individuals replacing their
corporeal pabulums for mental prisons
prisons tangible enough to be considered plausible
manifestations of substantiation
actualized from the terminologies of the human ability of
communication
this assiduous system of the privileged entitling a factitious
authority over the narrative of all afflicted ethnic groups
the arete of said people becoming misconstrued under the
pusillanimous system of our oppressor ideology of emolument
forcing those groups of people to abscond their brilliant
traditions and ideas for the equanimity and melioration of
their core existence as a whole
though the existence of history defines the advent of systems

such as american appropriation and other atrocities as actualities
its apocryphal of recondited abstraction remains disguised within certain products of all cultures....

○ **Dictionary** ●

Amorphous ◦• lacking definite form; having no definite shame; formless.
Arete ◦• the aggregate of qualities, as valor and virtue, making up good character.
Assiduous ◦• constant; unremitting.
Deontology ◦• ethics, especially that branch dealing with duty, moral obligation and right action.
Enucleate ◦• to remove from its enveloping cover.
Equanimity ◦• mental or emotional stability or composure, especially under tension or strain; equilibrium.
Erudition ◦• knowledge acquired by study, research etc.; learning.
Factitious ◦• not spontaneous or natural; artificial.
Indefatigable ◦• incapable of being tired out; not yielding to fatigue; untiring.
Mucilaginous ◦• adhesive.
Nostrum ◦• a scheme, theory, device, etc., especially one to remedy social or political ills.
Pother ◦• a heated discussion, debate, or argument.
Pusillanimous ◦• cowardly
Quandary ◦• a state of perplexity or uncertainty, especially as to what to do.

Recondite ∘• dealing with very profound, difficult, or abstruse subject matter.

Xenophilic ∘• an attraction to foreign peoples, cultures, or customs.

Amaranthine Apologue

A Story of Terrene and its Sapiens of Recapitulation Pt. 4:

The Anatomic Liberation of

The Existential Paradox Symbiote

lost.

adrift in the aphotic expanse
an autogenous mentiscape embarks on an inchoate journey
its path steered by the enigmatic forces of kismet.
within this realm it seeks illumination
guided by the faint whispers of prognostication
foretelling of a transformative enlightenment.
as its quest evolves
drifting
in the penetralia of its nascency
the mentiscape descries the outlines of obscured truths,
revealing revelations previously veiled in shadows.
the effulgence of a brilliant light
refracting a nascent existential aspiration
into an ephemeral spectrum
shaped of
dumbbells
clovers
donuts
and spherical miracles
a prismatic spectacle
evinces
the mentiscape

acknowledging the vast expanse of a known unknown
confronts the vicissitudinous nature of its nescience
in a moment of quiescence
it finds strength
its resolve steeled by the trials endured
wielding the power of the effulgence
the mentiscape takes form
delving deeper into the mysteries of its existence
in the stillness of respite and reflection.
challenges recrudesce
the echos of retrograde forgoing evolutive
echoing of wisdom loss
another fleeting memoriter of its remembrance
another fleeting memoriter perpetuating the lie
engulfing the once mentiscape
now
of a brain-dead mortal of emotion

a certainty remaining
the effulgence of the existential paradox symbiote

the End of part 1

○ **Dictionary** ●

Ambulate ∘• to walk about or move from place to place.
Aphotic ∘• lightless; dark.

Autogenous ∘• self-produced; self-generated.

Descrying ∘• to see (something unclear or distant) by

looking carefully; discern; espy.

Effulgence ·• a brilliant radiance; a shining forth.

Ephemerality ·• the quality or condition of being ephemeral.

Inchoate ·• not yet completed or fully developed; rudimentary.

Kismet ·• of ancient egyptian principalities; ancient egyptian religion.

Memoriter ·• by heart; by memory.

Mentiscape ·• "mentiscape," is a portmanteau (a combination of words/meanings, blended to form a new word), combining "mentis," (latin word for "mind" or "mental,) with "scape,"(a suffix used in english to denote a scene or a view) suggesting a landscape of the mind, evoking imagery of a vast, intricate terrain of thoughts, feelings, and mental processes.

Nascency ·• beginning to exist or develop.

Nescient ·• lack of knowledge; ignorance.

Penetralia ·• the innermost parts or recesses of a place or thing.

Prismatic ◦• of, relating to, or like a prism.

Prognosticative ◦• to forecast or predict from present indications or signs; prophesy.

Quiescence ◦• being at rest; quiet; still.

Recrudesce ◦• to break out afresh, as a sore, a disease, or anything else that has been quiescent.

Retrograde ◦• moving backward.

Vicissitudinous ◦• a change or variation occurring in the course of something.

Echoes of Autoionization

the annuna GODS who created me probably started slavery because greed doesn't beget greed in their north american wet dream as they capitalize off of their end game o● frodo was our beginning we lost our beginning as esmaralda the interracial bethesda

thine retrograde is impending enucleated in prime we're metroid with the echoes of autoionization our encephalons steadily pacing our corporality matrix amazing our first plantation was cajon mixed with summation prevaricating to metian nations equivocating our vegetative duration immured in their legislation

trichotomous in the body of pyramidal astrology amphibolous to all gga and ge arteries they be calling me deracinated from all apology forget their ecology resurrecting from our astronomy GODS before antediluvian folk lore the kinds that promote wars shit lies and craft time on our dimes

Pangea's of Tabula Rasa ∘• Sapiens of Recapitulation

anamnesis is the thesis

its ideals of a contemporaneous nature formulate mere

statistical probabilities of a predestined existence

a protean constant of an anfractuous intendment

isochronal vibrations fragmented its once plenary composition

efficacious in the allocation of a new terrene

the moira of men ∘• triturating compounds amalgamate

coalescing encephalon's of imprisoned corporality's in which

their prosopopoeial beliefs are originated ∘• such a wager of

faith and credulity in a deity of a consequential unimportance

∘• a paradoxical being of the sapiens imagination

or does such plausibility lie in the minds of geriatric individuals

what of the risk then in that of an ancient order adjudicating

over the conforming masses

altruistic men of multifarious acreages live by the orders

machinated decrees ∘• manipulated by their casuistic

stratagems

tenacious in its peregrination of ascendancy a pernicious
democracy and its jurisprudence anent a society of
apportioned foreignism
reigns terrors of a unitary supremacy upon the unaware
masses
powered by a preponderancy of benighted heirs and
plebeians
civilizations of acculturational asceticism within their
variegated sodalities are beguiled by the orders deceptive
actions
thus alluding to the de rigueur of the abstracted encephalon
the nascency of this mucilaginous vicissitude procreates a
confounding denouement in the hoi-po-loi of terraqueous
their ideological perspectivism's diluting the macro-cosmic
embodiment of their actualization ·• their schisms within self
contend with memoriter's of past replaced by retrograde
amnestic fallacies of alienation ·• thus pangea's conflicted
coalescence of its abstraction and its celestial's past and
future bear reflective properties of its sapiens of

recapitulation

Also From Author

Cinquefoil Buds of the Spring Summery Ai and the Renaissance of the Epistemophile

as we glide with poise towards the zenith of cassio

our perennial bud petals make shortstop in the cynosure of egitto

a hidden meadows past once frozen from the frigid winter

now thawed from the vestiges of the approaching spring

a destination that's far from home | a home that's far from complete

and yet still here we are

amidst the foliage we tried to remember

a foliage that knew of our origination | a foliage that knows of our demise

hyperborean mortals of this new world speak of a young desdemona

enigmas of the sepulcher beneath what we land upon

containing the anamnesis of her fable | a fable thought lost

her stem riven from prior betrayals

her smell still that of a flowery rose | her salubrious physique still mesquite

every branch of who she was to become

now a mild topiary made of a lesser imagery

death of a caged bird | obsolescence of we

spring falls

summery of a colder winter to come

a colder winter for some but ineluctable to all

same visions of hope

cruelest now is our world

how now we all forgo our enemies | how now we all forget ourselves

from our innate understandings of our external corporeality's

◆ Lo√ K3 nowledge ◆

to our reprobate halves split tween satyagraha and our tandem ideations of

en-masse and autonomously affiliated energies

as our evolution arises from the buds we once were

to becoming a shimmering inanimate being within a dream incomplete

dissimulating our copse mind with their pseudo anatomic dreams of an organic reality

the fallacy | that the grass is greener on the other side of everything

komorebi personified permeating our gemütlich hibernaculum

with incipient emanations of another spring summery

the vitality of those beginning buds now effloresced

vying against the vibrant necrosis of macrosiphum rosae

and the long-awaited conclusion to septem circumstantiaes answer

of why

Danseuse

lost dreams of your old republic

dreams of decrepit buds from the torrid corrosion of the gilded sunrise

again now ready to spring anew

dancing at the first glance of the thawing wintertide

as their new memories begin to form amid the glaring of a stars first arrival

avoiding the fall that their empiric minds of past once hid behind

Zodiacal Aureole |
Diametrical Cranes of Astrology |
Virgo of the Autumnal Wintertide |
The Horologium Stargazer |

astraea
winged goddess
zeus's decree
methodical scales of virginity and mercury
telluric polarities of negative and femininity
unsure of self but sure of one thing
claim to thine throne
carnelian incrusted
thanos of the gemstones
tellurian allured kaleidoscope
achromatic in self
practicality of emotional vibes reign supreme
mucilaginous holds of past stick tight
grasping a future ahead of present times
the you of now
make flight the fight
only slows you down
supreme being of the historic arts
anachronistic progenitor
knowledgeable of the start | aware of its middle | assuming the end
a pleasant clover of the astronomic belt
baring gifts of balance
to those void of the continuity of motherhood

and the extremity of mankind's everlasting loyalty

as mercury descends upon thee
ask yourself who will you become anew
when the actuality of nyastae creeps upon you

Make-Believe

a smile without a face
mental conception

lonely is the world that i slept with
alone is the fervent emotion that crept in

your imagery personified
in it
i can sense your manifest
i'm hoping that you too
can sense my innocence

hoping that you can sense you
the you outside of the you in me
hoping that you too can make me believe

in the make-believe

–the fiction that becomes their realities

Ikebana | Peacherino Flowers of the Rarefied Symposium

the way that you've graced lo√e

the way that you lead

my central emporium

from selling abstractions of lust and greed

to physicality's of fragility and spiritualties in need

dionaea muscipula

behind the pain he wrought

a healing embrace behind the lo√e i bring

our truth of what becometh of we

seemingly bursting at the seams

of the flowerets second awakening

Me Myself and I

i was born into this world without faith or guarantees

without lo✓e | without hope | without passion or currency

all i ever had was my environment and shady figures

my family fractured right from the beginning so how you figure

i'd be able to give ya you myself and ties

best thing i could have given you girl was we | your lies | my pride

because you had an icebox inside

i wasn't let in

didn't help that i held the torch out of reach i helped cause the ending

no more newer beginnings

i hate that faulty narration

i hate interrogations

we knew one another so well and now we're both in this cell

steady investigating old messages

old events that seemed so suspicious when even if it happened we

go about fixing the bad with bad intentions and smile when we really feel sad beneath the surface

i'm glad that we're both hurting because the only thing we could have given each other that we never had was trust and honor and there isn't honor amongst secrecies

no trust in us honest thieves

no lo✓e for just you and i

no room for truth in those jaded lies

no space for us inside of my pride

we both met at me myself and i

which led to us | your lies | my pride

then we got ourselves together

and now it's us

our death revived

Rovaniemi

road trips like this let me reflect

that time i spent with you i had to deflect

your heart was mine and that i couldn't protect

i wouldn't protect

i was to worried about guns and butter

having enough of us but not enough experience

i was the runt of my litter

you know matrices of the privileged and bitter

mother did everything to run away from our family ties

left my father behind with his family and pride

his recreational energy led to brothers and sisters that i never knew

more fragmented pieces on this rubik's cube

stuck with moms until i die

maybe she sees the him in i

my family ties shit they cut themselves

they left me scarred mentally

like i'm supposed to do this love thing all on my own

like i don't need you

love of my life sometimes i'm see through

unappreciative of everything you are and everything that you do

because if i get hurt then that's on me like it was on her

the streets you claim i could have been a part of

but this lo✓e inside saved me from that

and manifested a sudden indifference out of these friends who claimed

friend and lo✓ers alike

because they were all the same

their prices to fame being not dying alone inside

my price to fame was to recreate this confounding imagery

of moms and pops with wedding rings and bells that ring loudly amongst the dead and alive

so many of my family has died

they were to heartbroken to continue

loneliness was their skin of shame | necrosis for external hides

my skin of shame was my heart on my sleeve

hunger was in my soul

but the pain was to vibrant for you to comprehend

being hurt for you was a new pain

orgasmic as the needle to your skin that imbues pain

but honestly my honesty is second to none

though my ego stands the test of time

my prides a zombie that comes alive at inopportune times

im sure that in some way it's hereditary

and you wonder why we could never work

why i can write about right ways to ease the hurt | to chill the burn

to blow out the candles of past and become that better me

that me that's healed for you and everything you need me to be but that's your vision that manifests from the pain inside

instead of dealing with the bad of me and leave

you rather churn the bad into good

turn the truth into lies | turn your heart solid inside

i was your scapegoat

you chased that fairytale of we inside of me

but i'm not chasing blame | the blame is dichotomous

accountability is key

cards on the table

i showed you mine from the beginning but where were yours

this lo✓e thing feels like escobar season

nowhere to run too | nowhere to hide

nobody to tell you the truth

only snakes left to confide in

roll the dice and hope the snakes that you ride with are either

venom-less or their fangs sharp enough to numb the tide of war

emotions left on the floor

no more commitments

cheaters walk through the door

diseases in the atmosphere

heartbreaks the new experiment

got to hurt to learn how to lo✓e again

black on black hues in lo✓e

without leaders in their prime to shine light on the lo✓e inside

to shine light on how to survive

i shined light on you and i

you shined light on only you

it's a battle before winning

but i've been there | as bad as i am

competition with us

that's isn't equity

and getting what we want when we want

that's not empathy | we need sympathies

im sorry you know how i am

when i'm writing with this pen

i share everything all at the same time

you got to understand my hurt to see that im not of a sane mind

we're not of the same minds

i understand that you lo√e me but us was more of my thing

i just didn't have the pieces from my unfortunate history to

complete our dream

instead i saw lust in what i've seen and not what i knew

i wish i knew what i know now

finally here in rovaniemi

The Black Mamba ♡ Ermias Asghedom
Tears of the Acronical Progenitors
and the Cimmerian Woes of Their Votaries

anachronistic progenitors that never die
prophesize abiogenetic ideologies
sporadic spontaneity of their manifest
as we are on the court | as we are in the booth
as we shoot our shot | as we spit our truths
and truth of death is relevant
histograms of our leaders murdered in their primes
governmental?
regular street mentality temperamental
enough to take his life? | enough to end his flight?
the plights of abstracted demons we never create but face
the struggles of black on black | liquor and guns | drug infested | division
plights they could have ended | plights they would have ended
disconnected from your history and became suspended in the oppressor's matrix of an artificial reality
where our leaders be forever taken by their lies of abstraction

rip to all anachronistic progenitors
-     "not a rapper or a poet; i'm a poem"
(Nipsey Huss | e; crenshaw and slauson)

Motēuczōma
Pyramidal Dichotomies of the Ānidi
አንድ

black and white hues but together they saw in rainbows
mixed pigmentation •° summary of their past woes
summery regrets of the blackberry winter
constellations intervene
turned them into an astronomical dilemma
pyramidal sectors of a past •° present •° and •° future
sectors of a you •° me •° and we
supremacy •° division •° or team
lie •° cheat •° or dream
dichotomous is their scheme
lo√e or hurt •° pain or truth
live or die •° stagnant or elevation
unity in a barren wasteland
ānidi with the understanding of self
huleti in the chamber
sositi of their mind •° body •° and soul

together as they imagined it to be

Onomatopoetic Distinctions of Poetichà Elegiac
The Reanimation of Rosaceae Manque

death
a means to an end
easing those ethereal pains from which she could never escape
stuck in a loop forever amongst her quadripartite
lo√es spiritoso
birthing narratives of acceptance
and yet jealousy still arrives
now here you are
ectothermic in your struggle to replicate life
death emulating its antithesis
past memoriters begin taking flight
landing in meadows of orthopraxy
reanimating olden views and prior beliefs
price of flibbertigibbet
distractions becometh belle epoque in nature
forming technetronic guanxi
a new elemental of the digital aesthetic
where your purpose manifests ideological prisms of contemptus mundi
hurt from a past thought of but done away with
our coup de grâce of necessary evils
to counteract your endearment
to counteract your lo√e for her
what happened to just us four
what happened to just me and you
now penitent for it all

reminiscent abstraction of rosaceae buried deep
in the gramadoelas of where we self-identify
ankhs of immortality
vultures of representation
the mire of this drenched soil
becometh an irreversible calliblephary
staining the facets of your composition
rebranding the woman i lo√ed so deeply
in our beginning

death of manke
birth
of poetichà elegiac

ˈbətərˌflī

a summery dream of a you and i

orange blossom petals that land at her feet

they give me butterflies

alabastar is the attire

i am her secret admirer

but from afar

within springs summery

those petals that once were vivacious | now languid

as the feet that had once sheltered the petals fall

now oscillate from the serenity of falls dawn

about the author

Keyontaye Williams is a well-known poet in Baltimore, celebrated for his stirring verses that touch the hearts of all who hear them. Beyond his literary pursuits, he finds joy in being a devoted father to his cherished daughter. Currently, Keyontaye is on a journey of self-discovery and academic achievement at CCBC Community College, where he is diligently working towards his dream of becoming a doctor. His commitment to excellence is evident in his pursuit of certifications in computer science and pharmacy, showcasing his diverse talents and determination to succeed.

In addition to his academic endeavors, Keyontaye is deeply invested in his community, offering support and guidance to those in need. Whether he's lending a helping hand or offering words of wisdom, his kindness and empathy leave a lasting impact on those around him. As he continues to navigate the complexities of life, Keyontaye remains steadfast in his pursuit of knowledge and personal growth, inspired by his unwavering optimism and passion for making a positive difference in the world.

Made in the USA
Columbia, SC
03 October 2024

ca38909d-0766-439f-b130-b1ab4ad4d3fdR01